MANDALAS

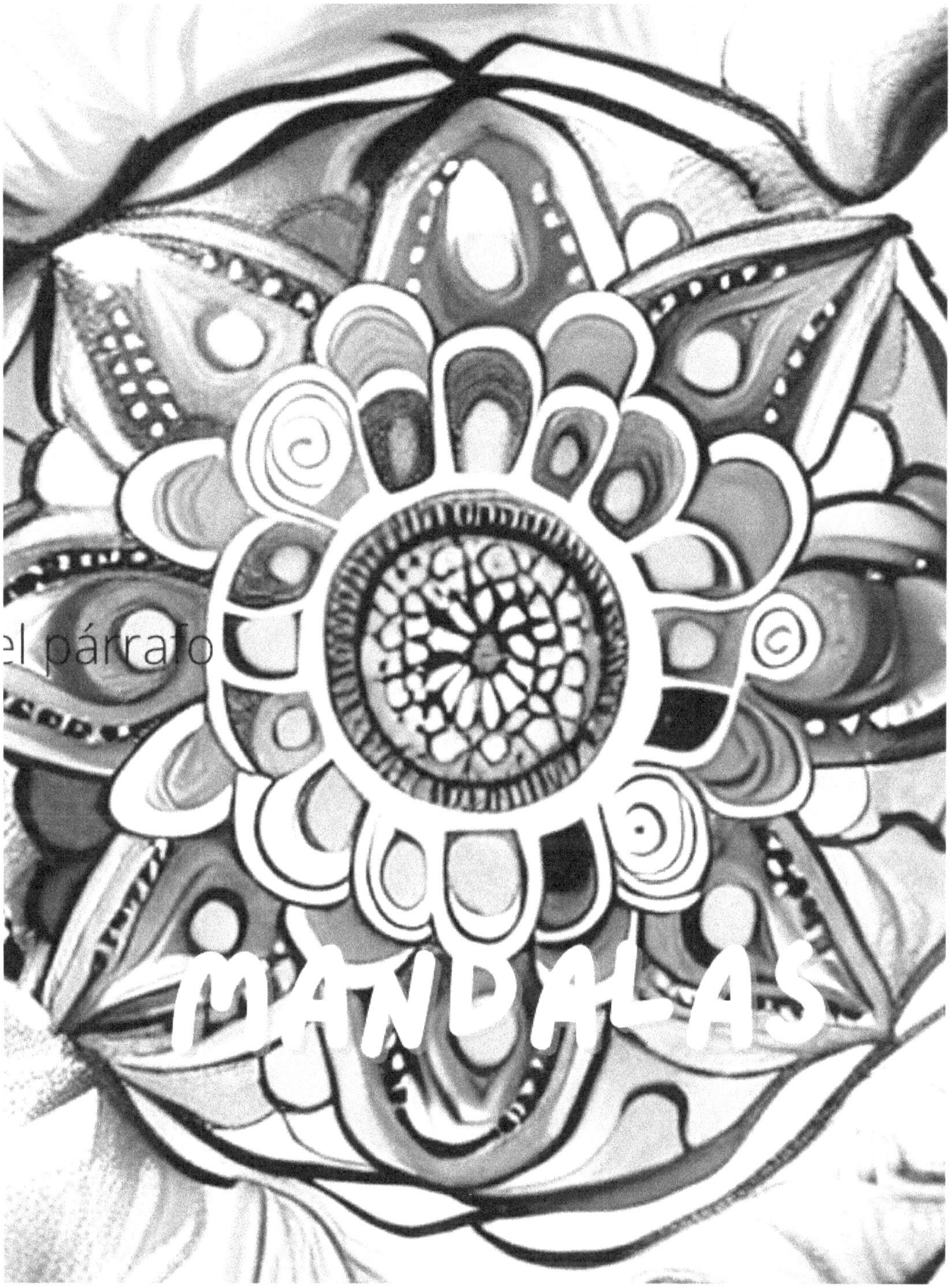

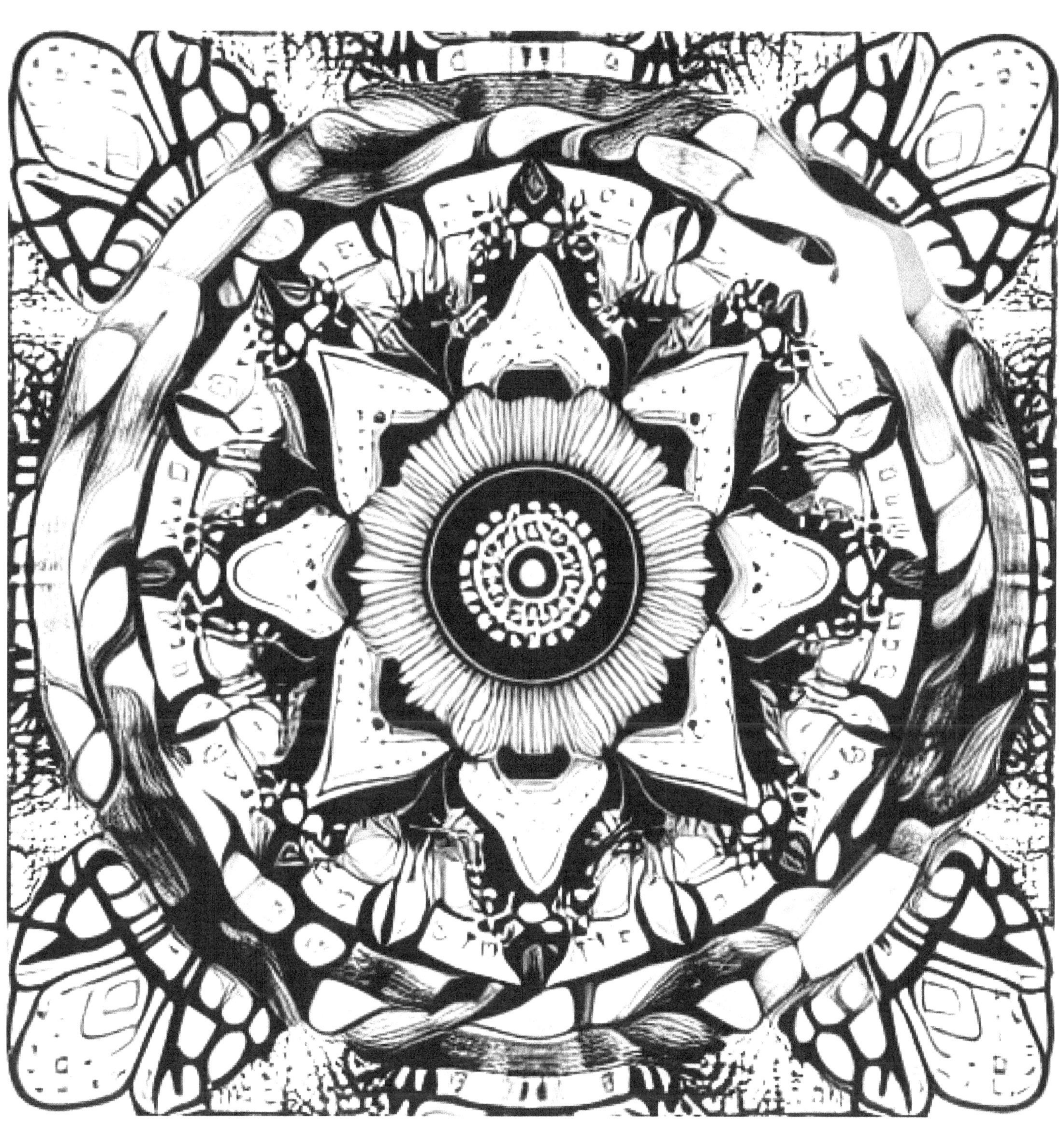

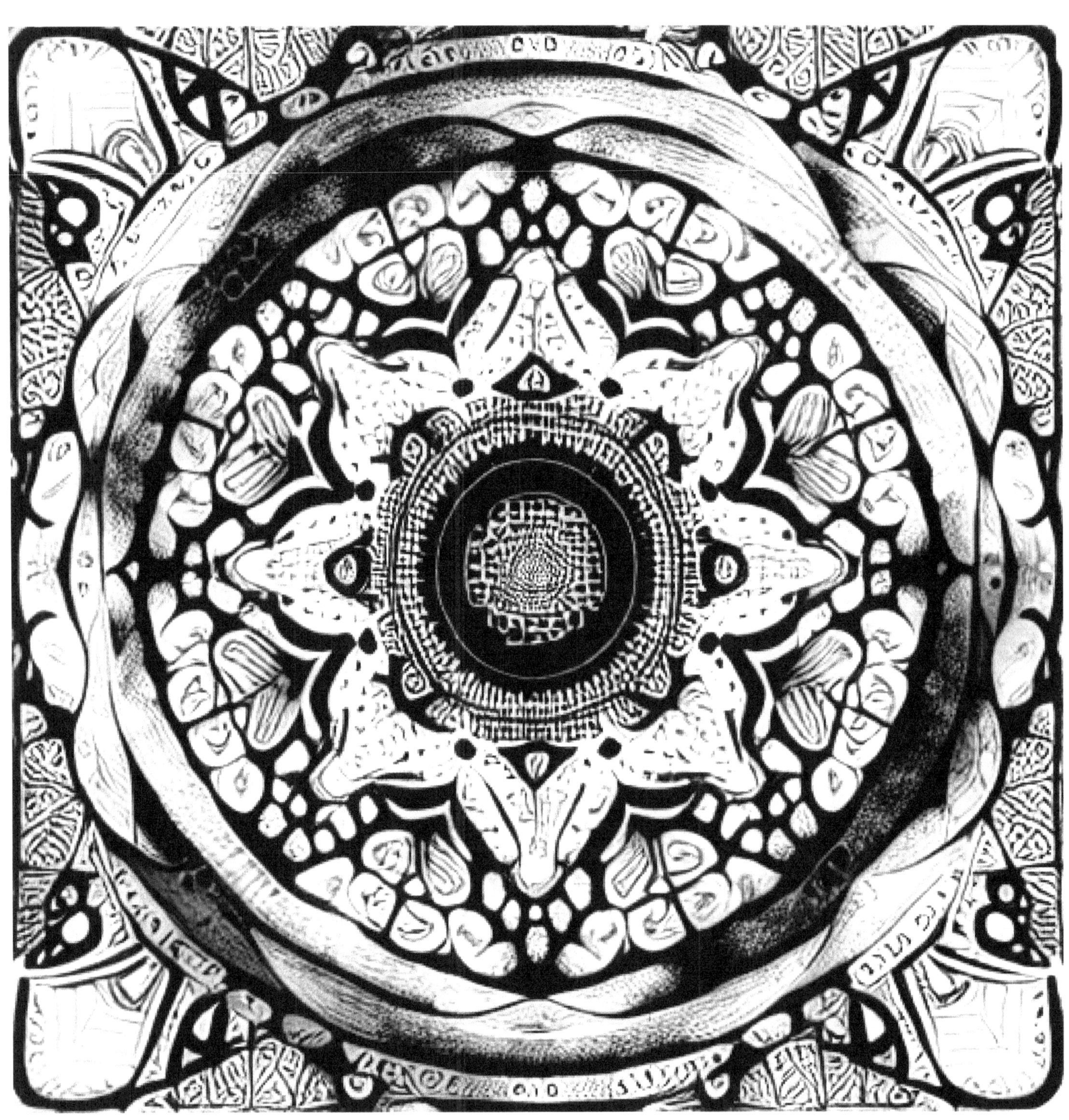

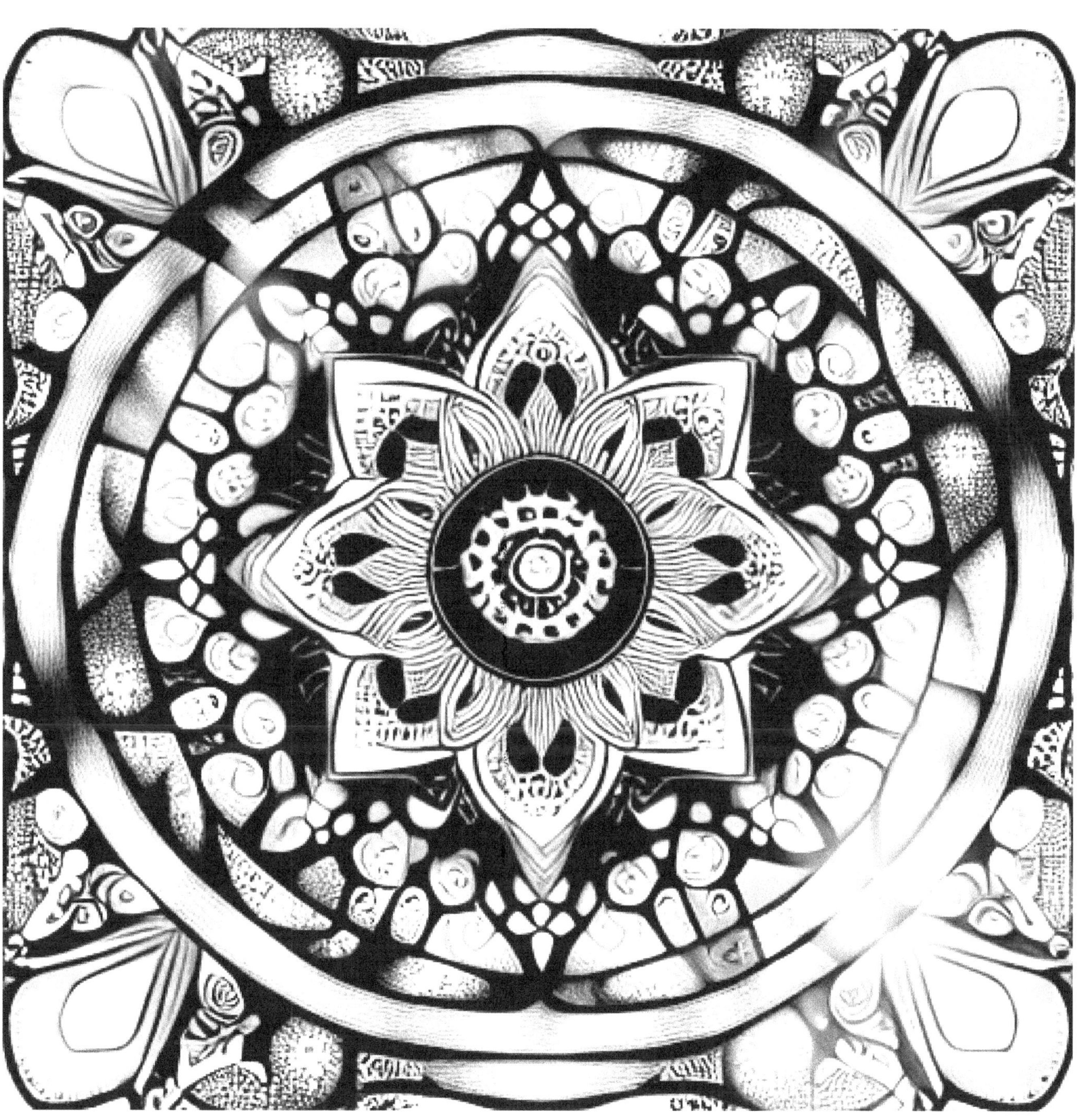

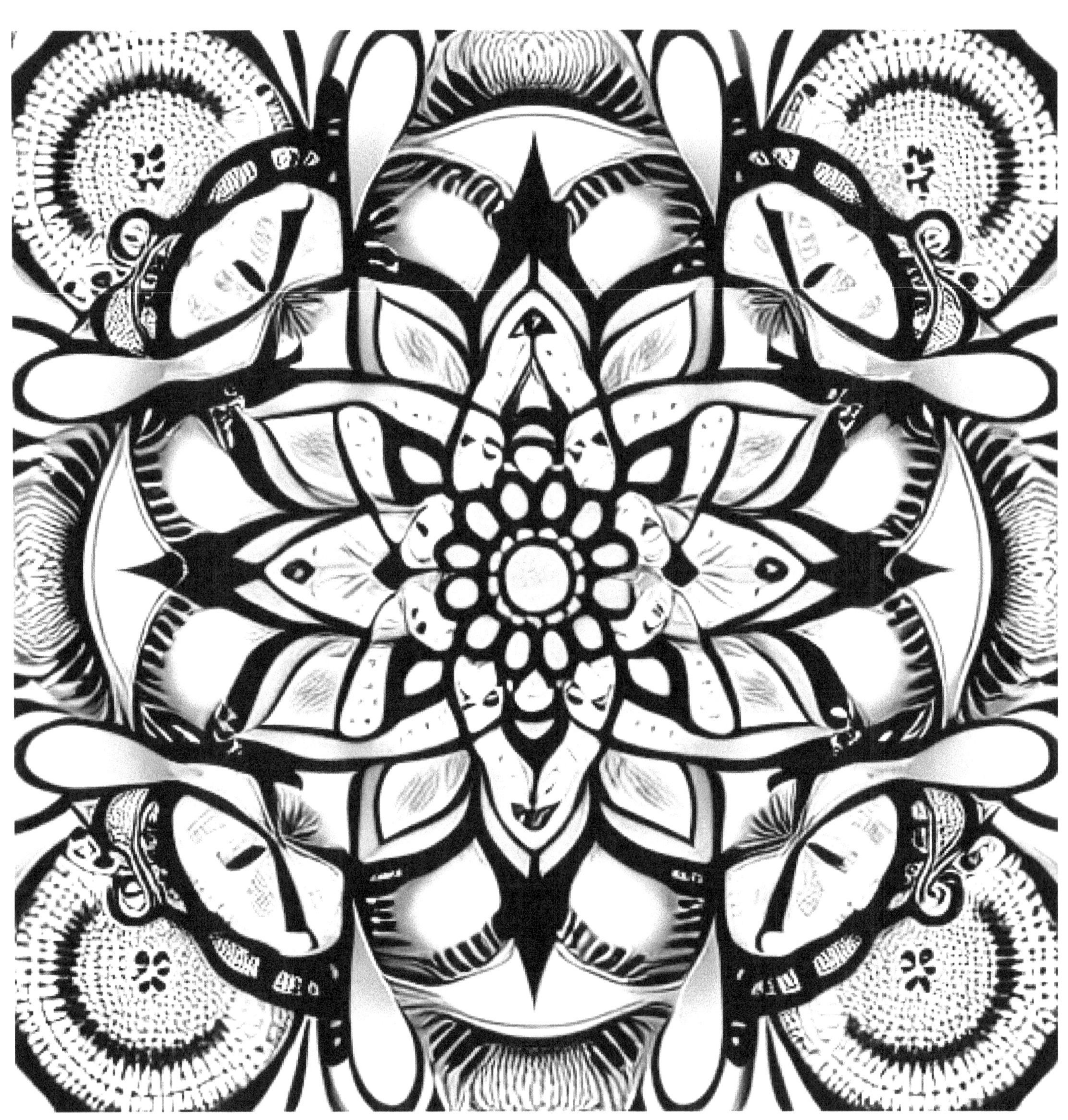

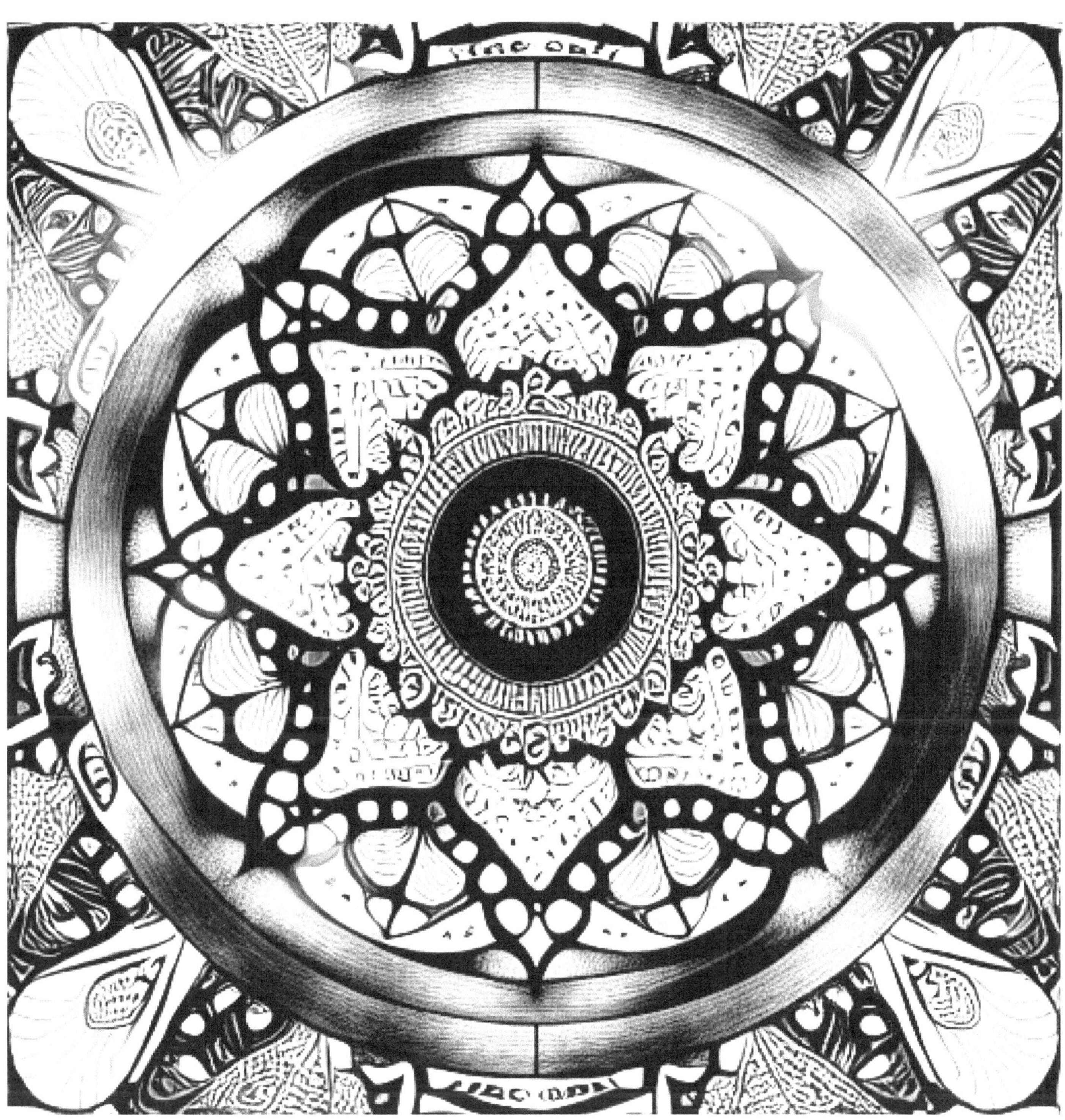

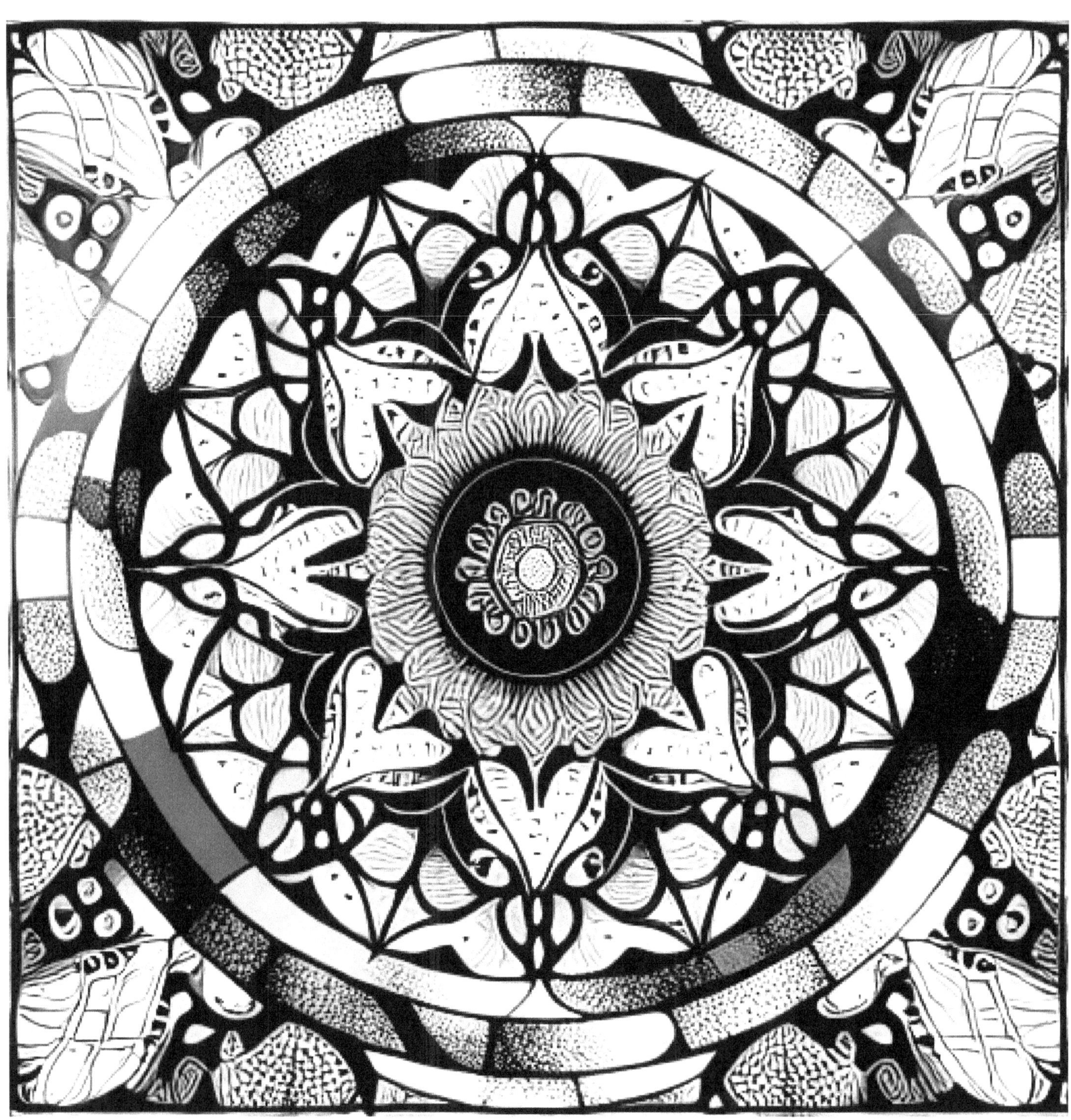

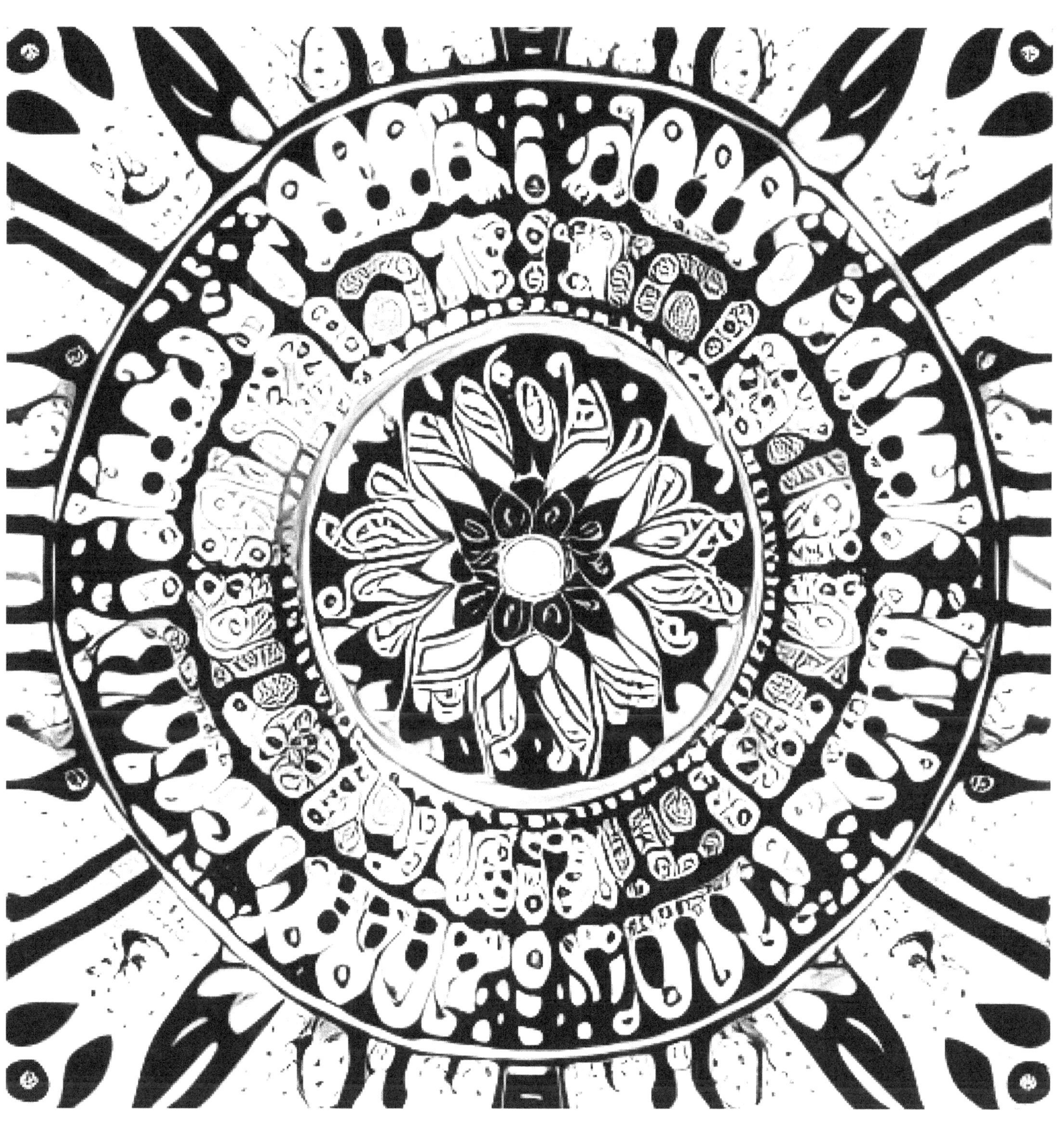

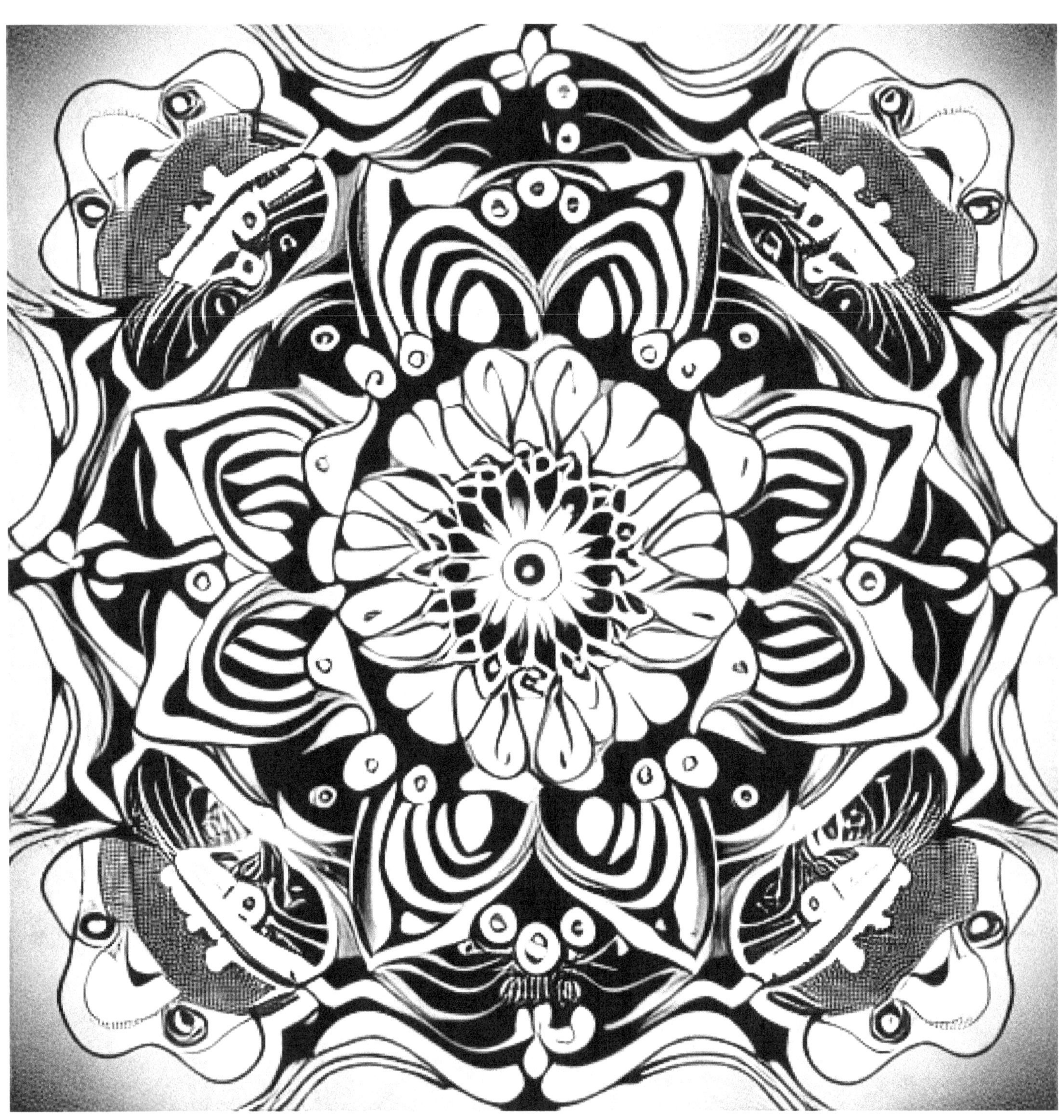

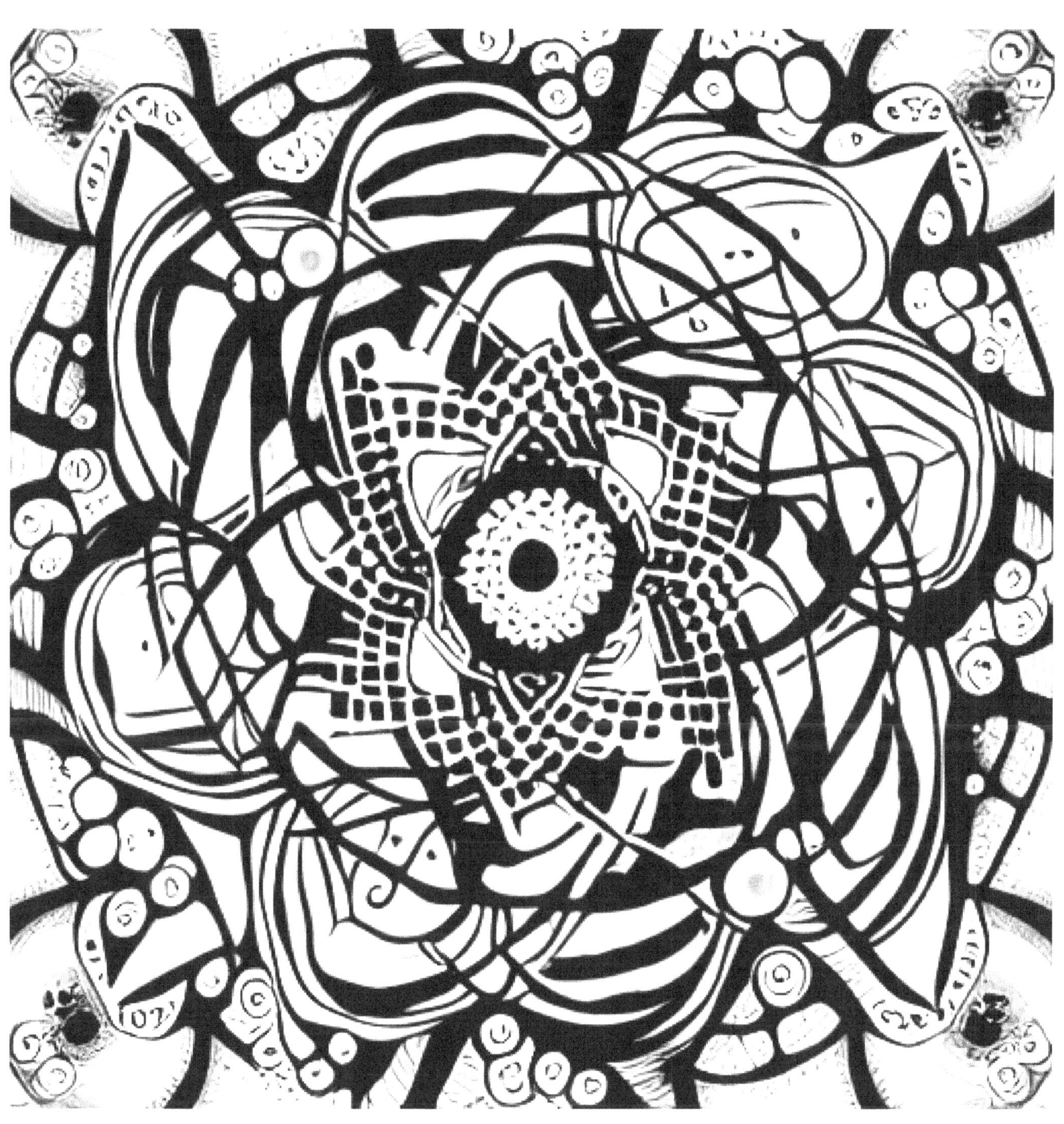

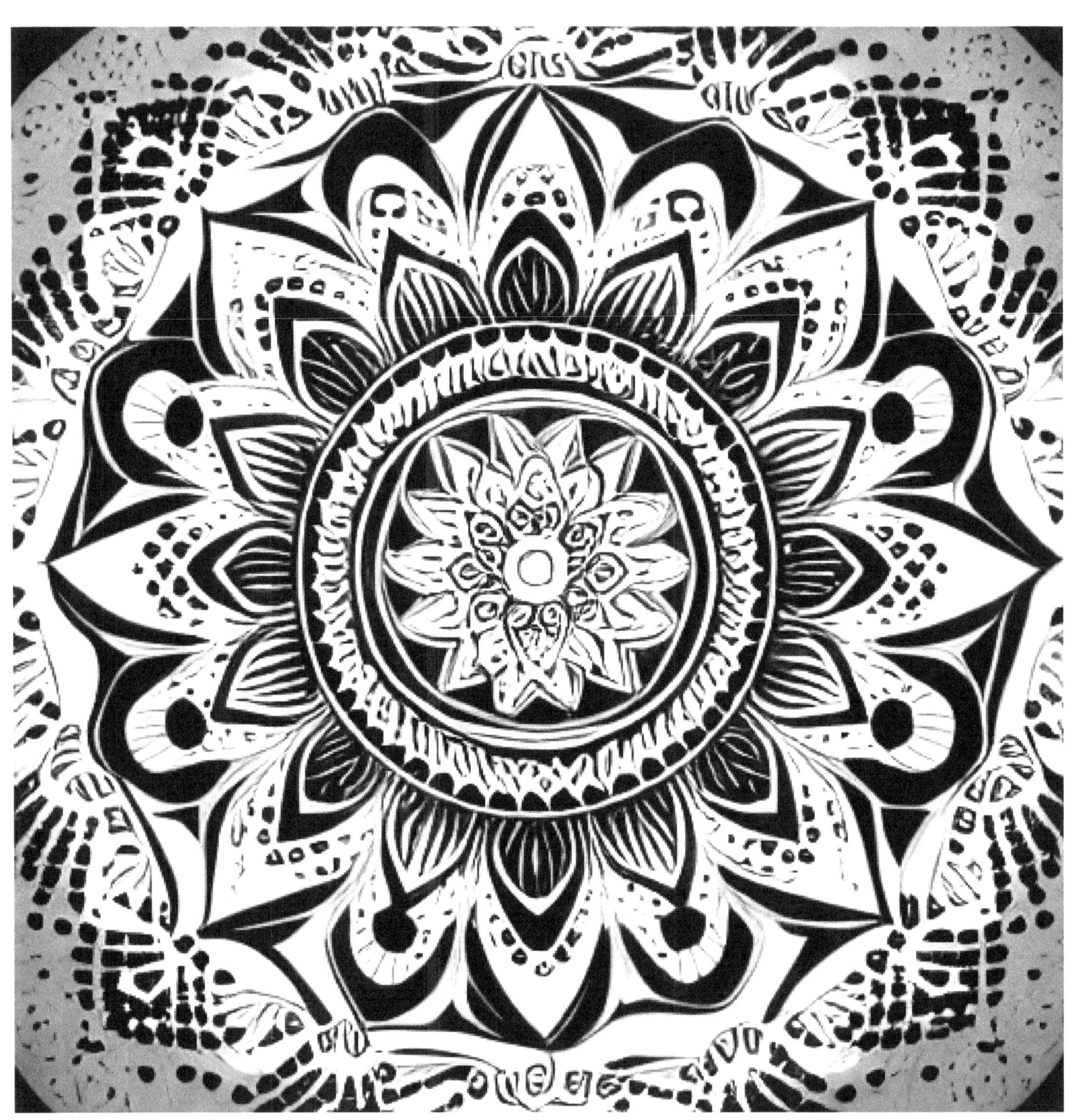

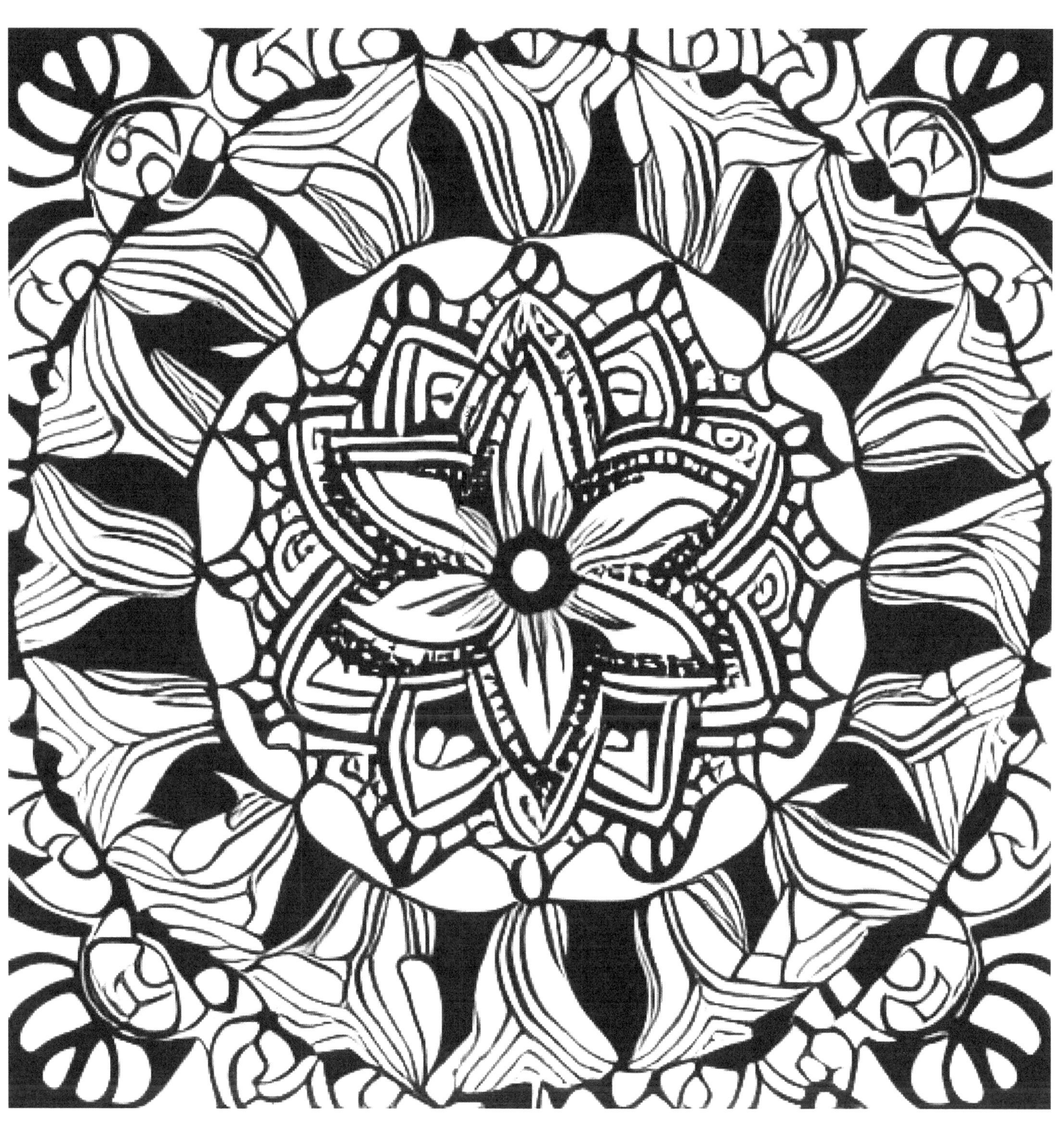

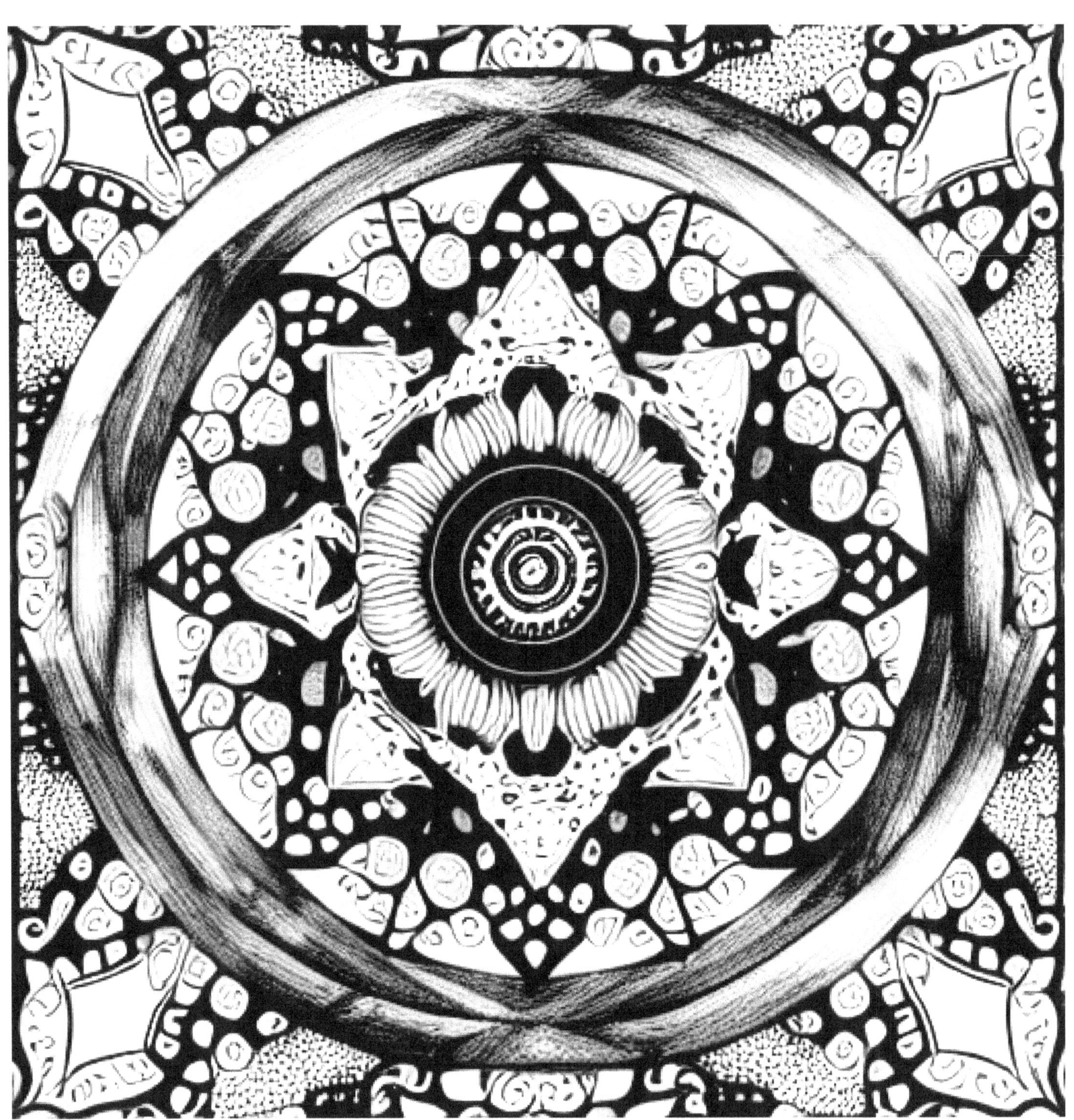

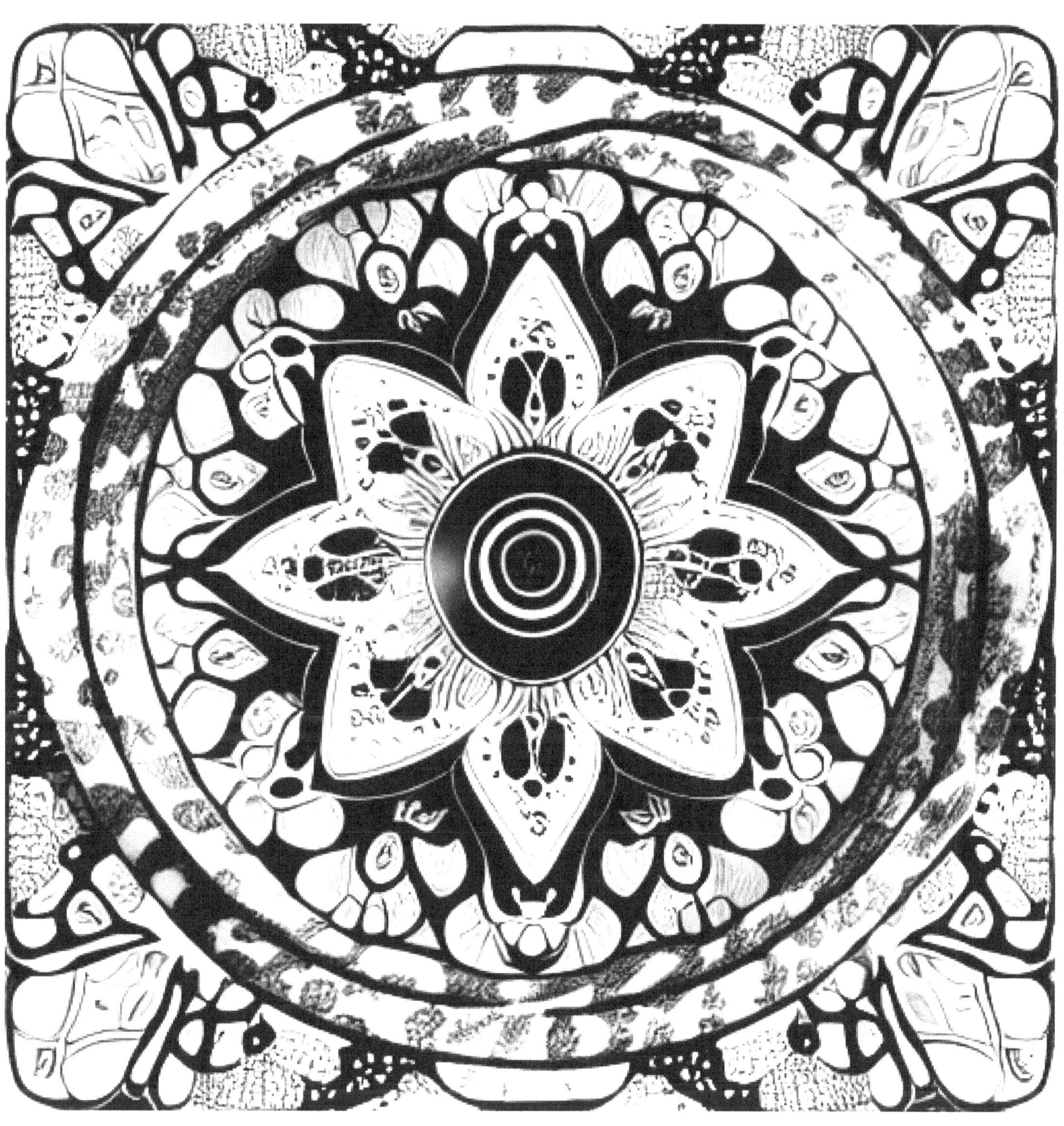

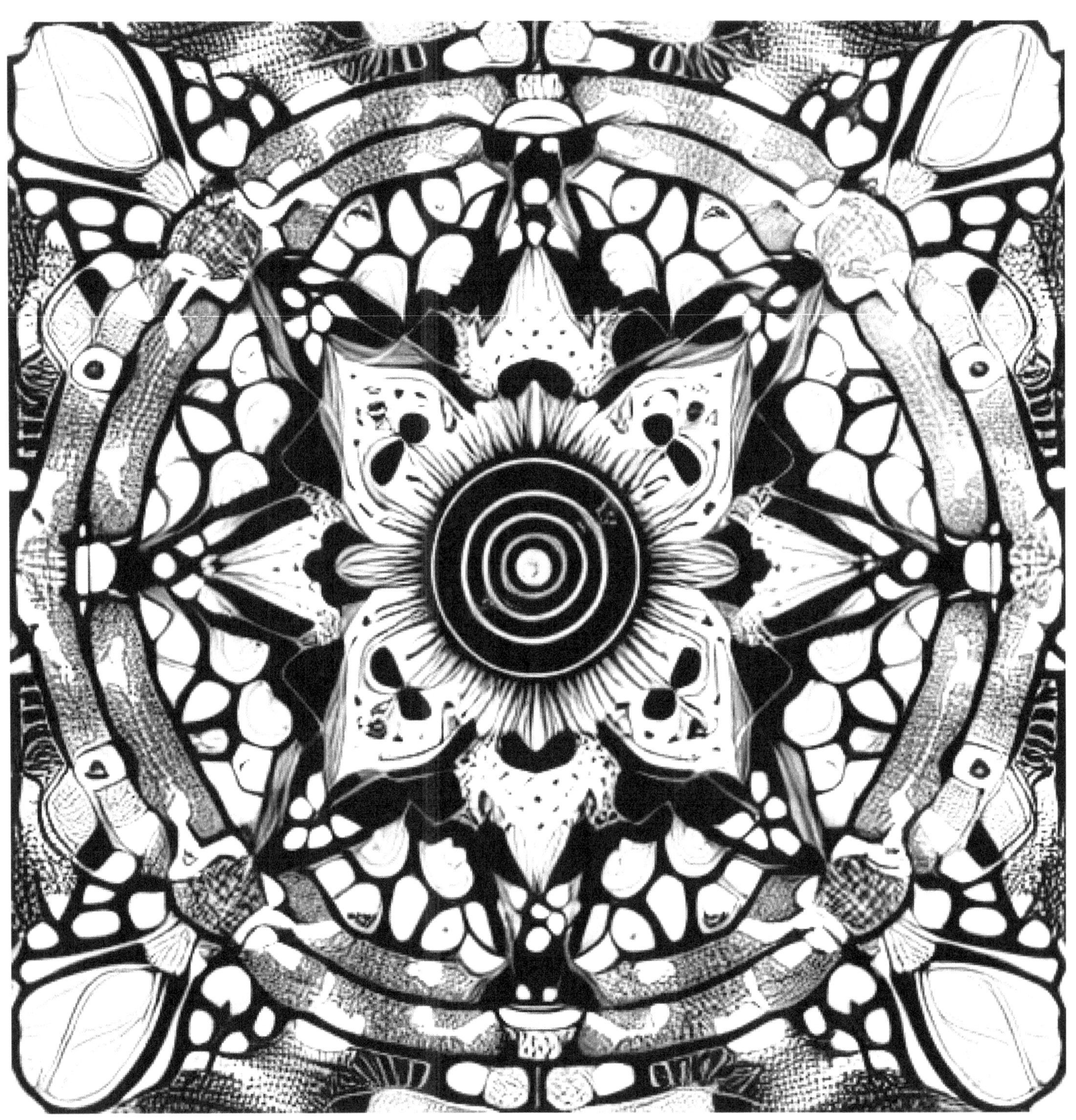

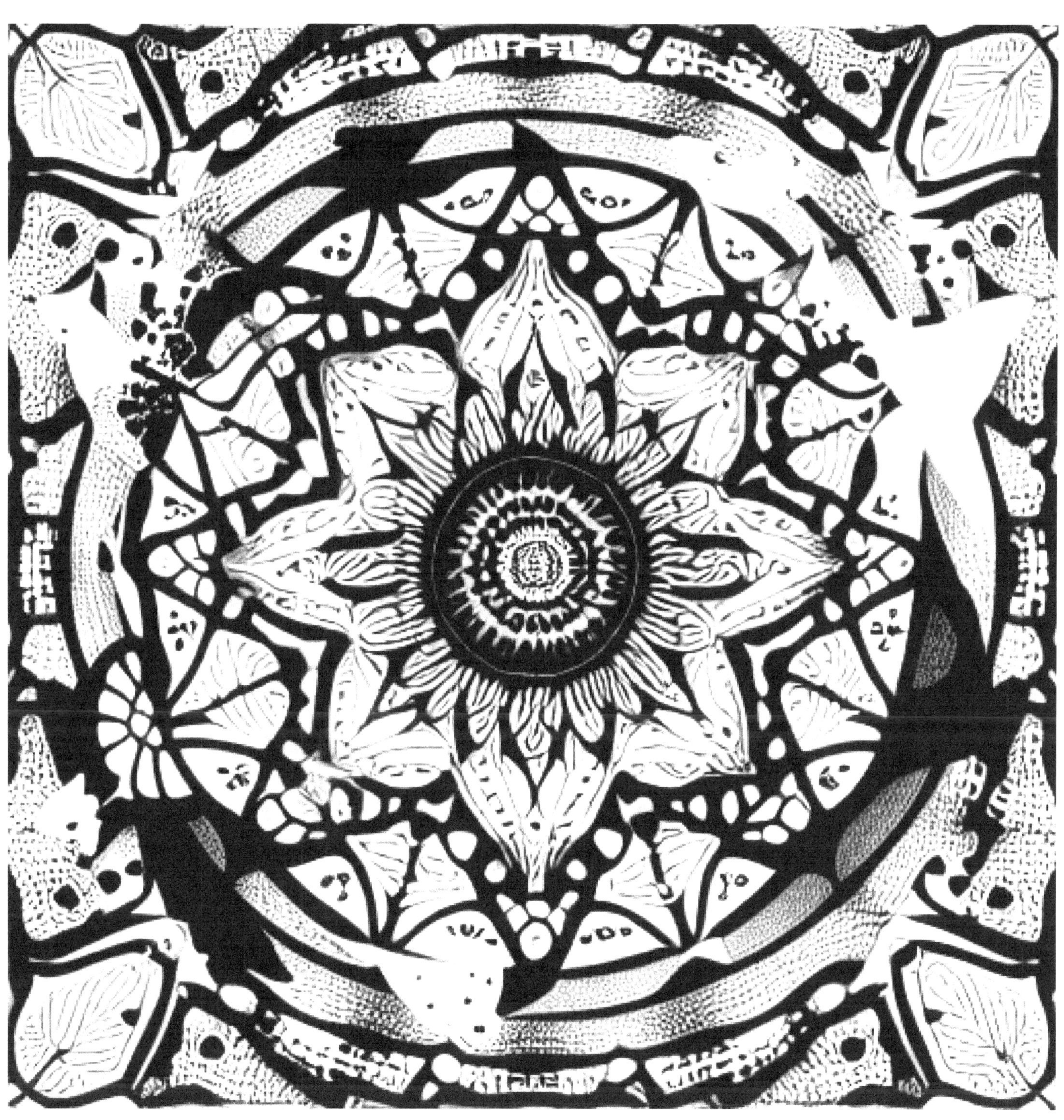

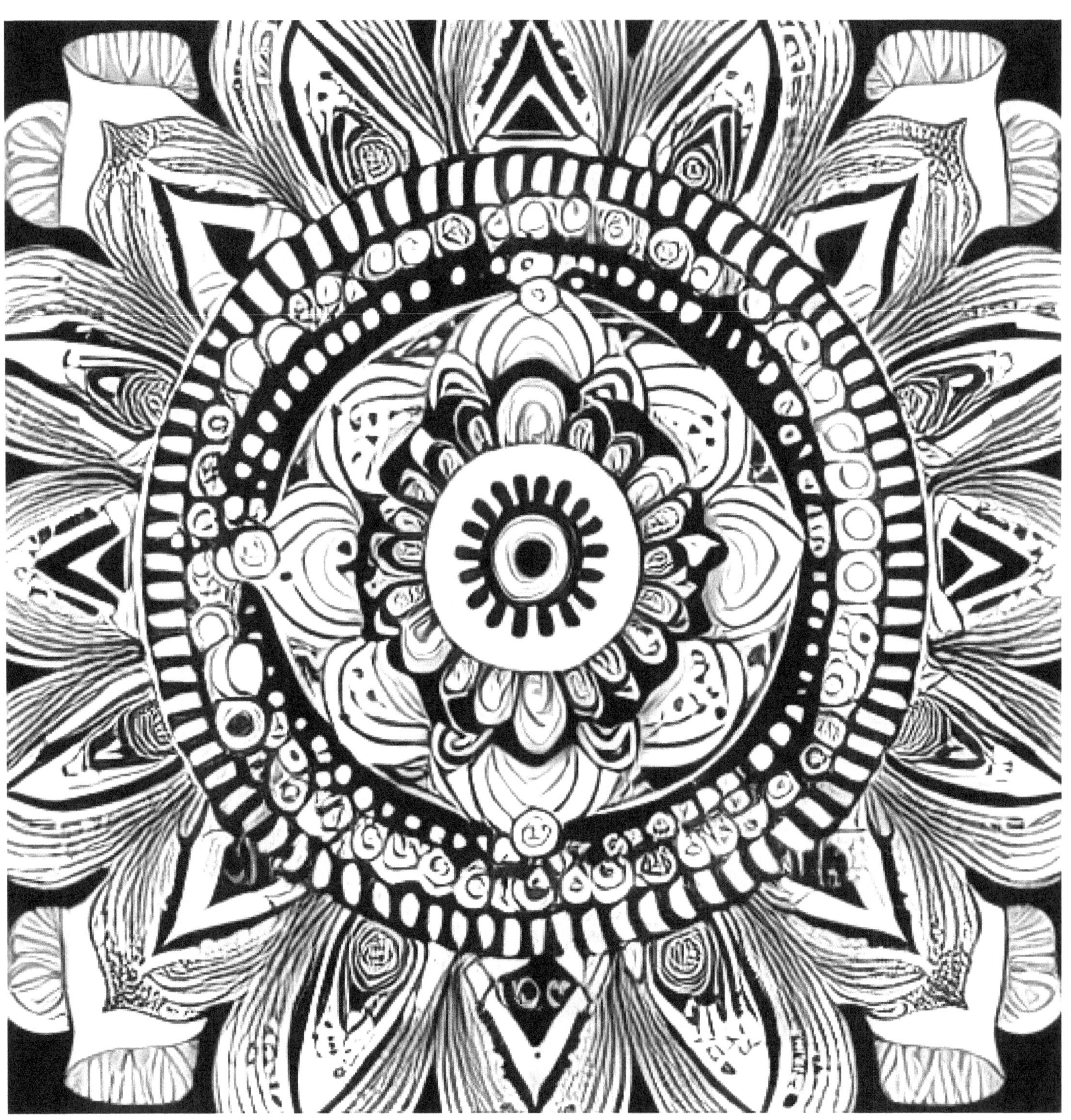

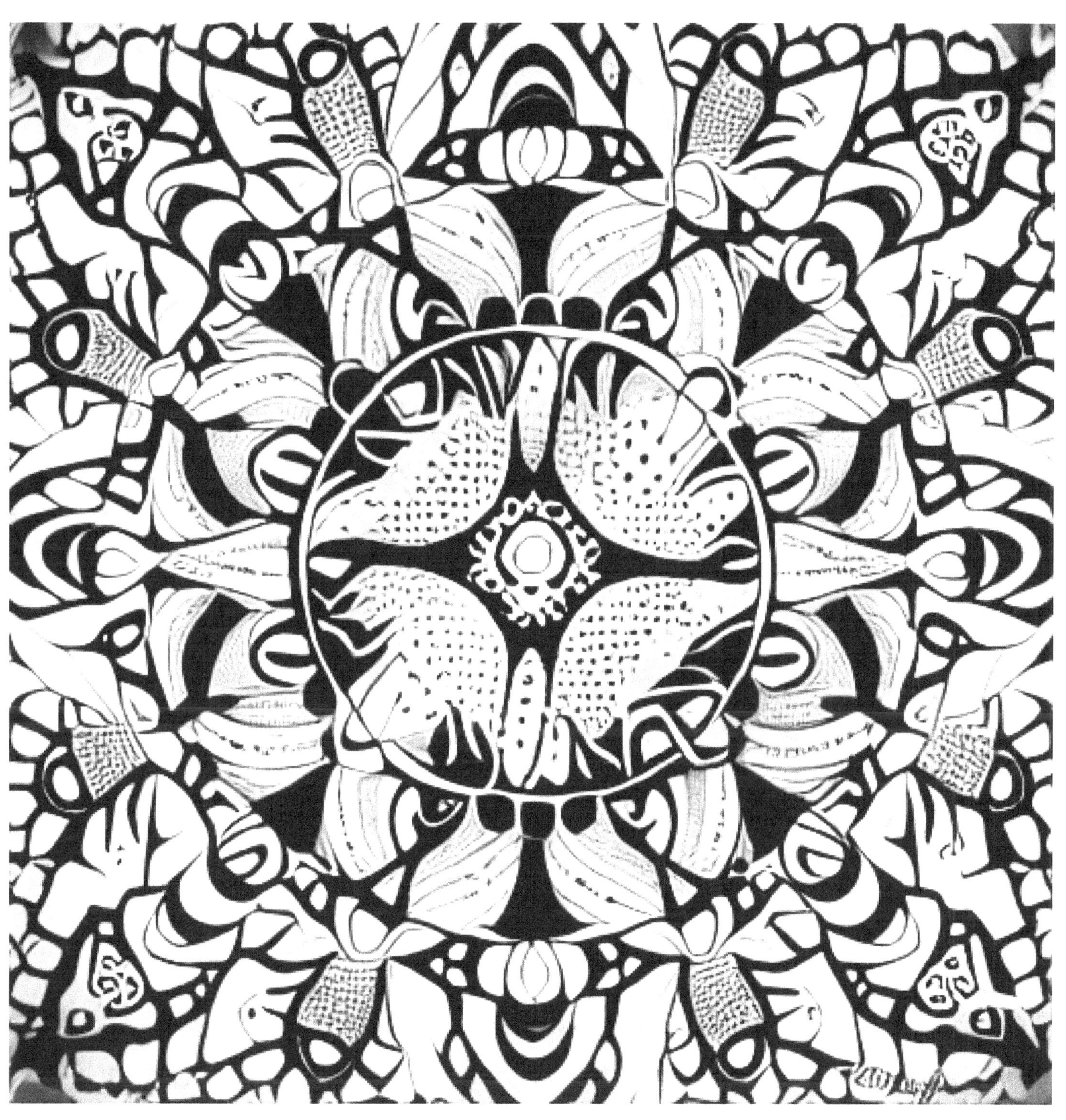

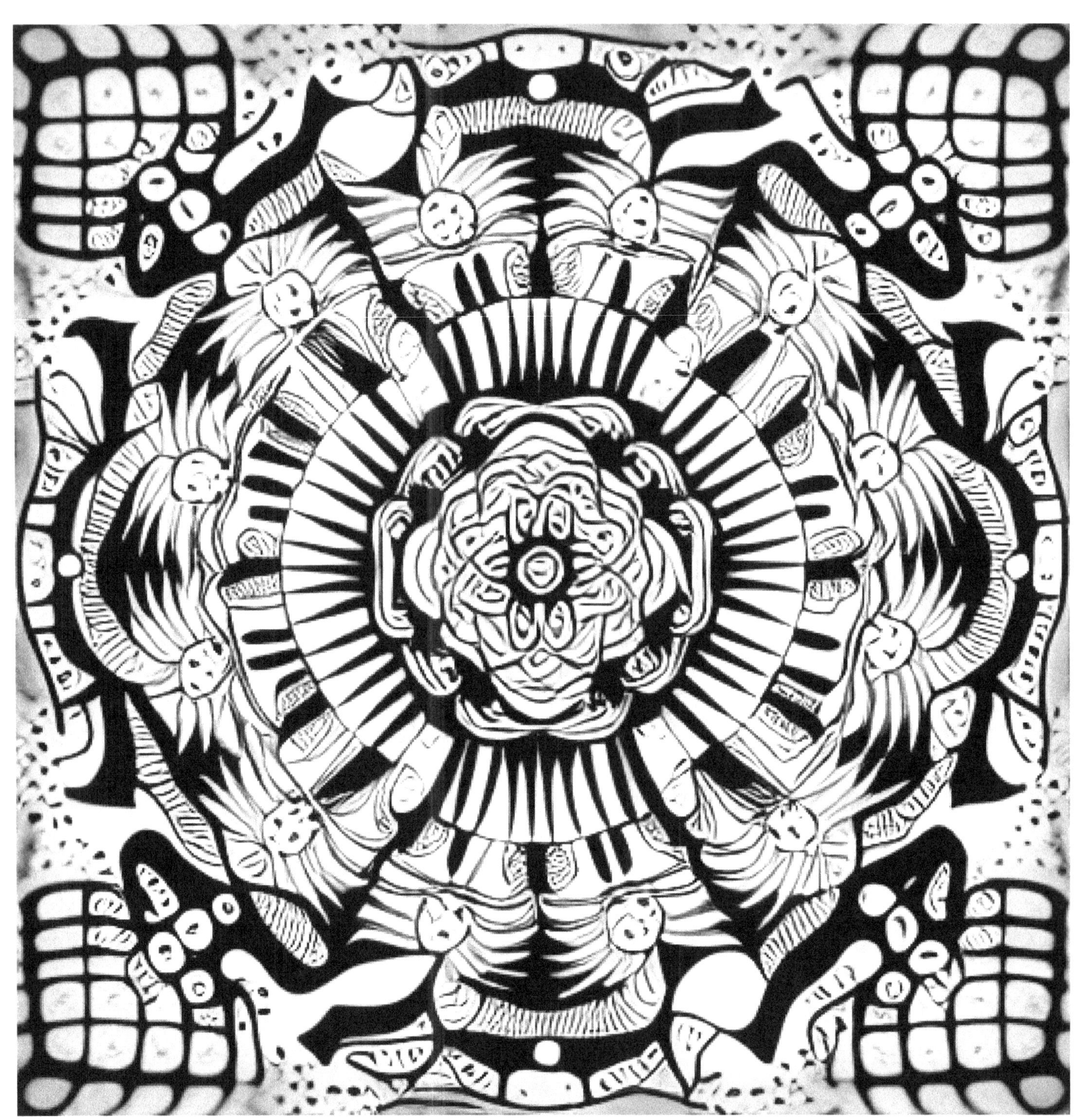

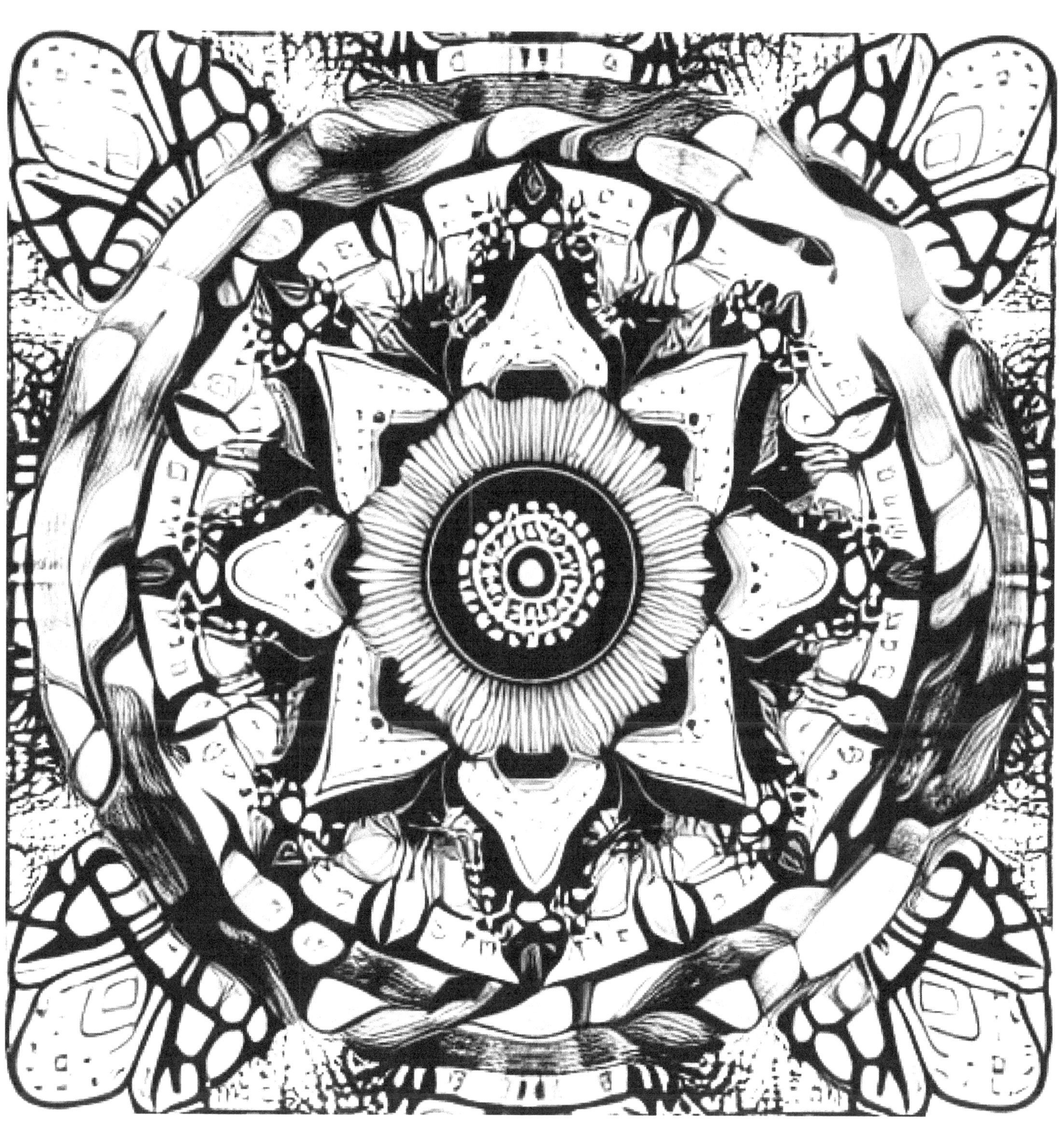

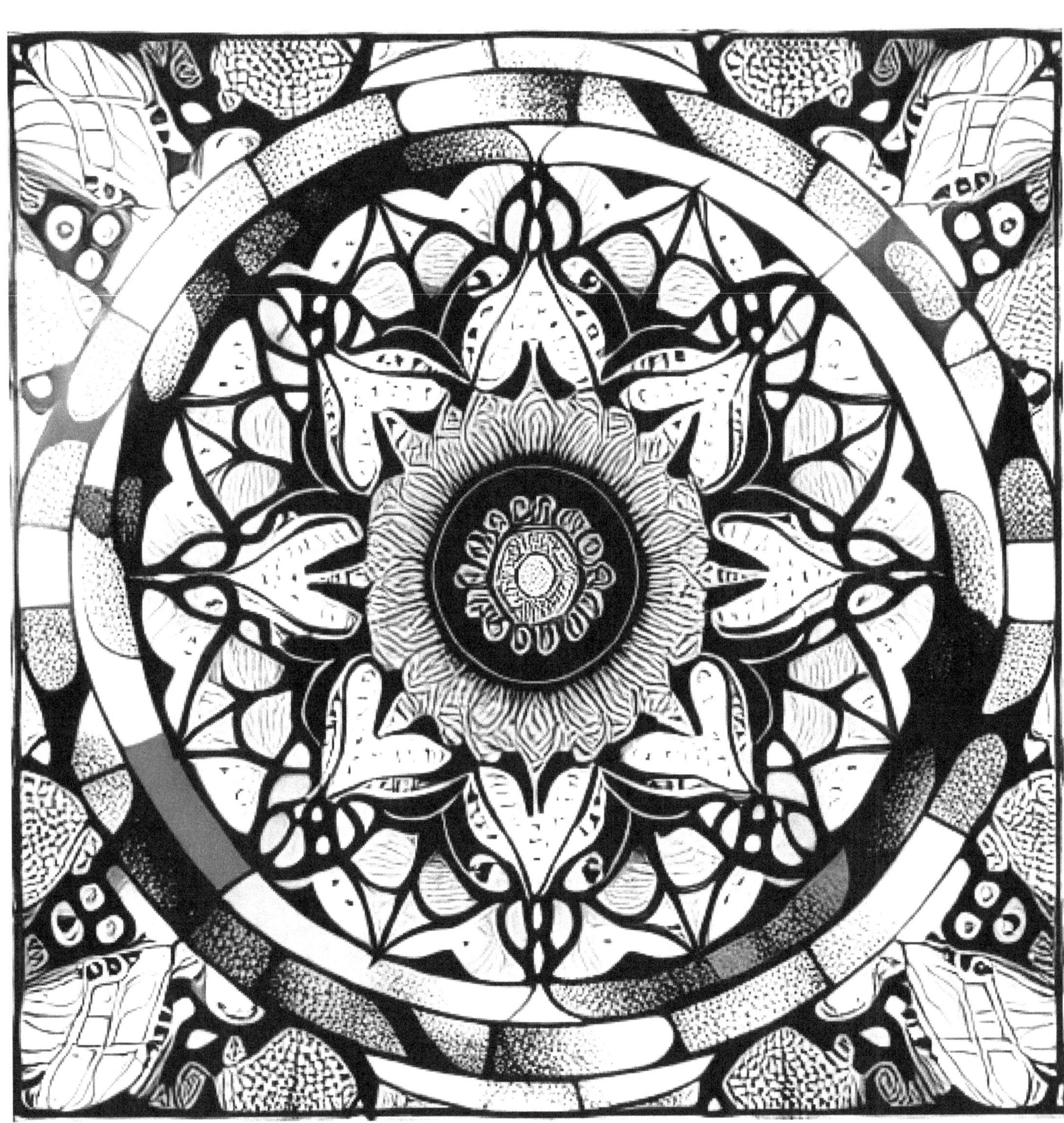

Conclusion

Thank you so much for purchasing this book. If you enjoyed it, then please leave an Amazon review. Reviews are the lifeblood of our publishing endeavors leaving a positive review would mean the world to us.